ABUNDANCE JOURNAL

A GUIDED JOURNAL TO HELP YOU
MANIFEST YOUR DREAMS.

ANNIE THE ALCHEMIST

Cover Art Copyright © 2024 by Annie Vazquez
Designed by Carolina Gonzalez and Flor Ana Mireles

1st Edition | 01
Paperback Pink Edition ISBN: 979-8-9895551-4-7

First Published March 2024

Published by Indie Earth Publishing

Also Available In:
Paperback Blue Edition ISBN: 979-8-9895551-6-1

For inquiries and bulk orders, please email:
indieearthpublishinghouse@gmail.com

Printed in the United States of America   1 2 3 4 5 6 7 8 9

Praise for Annie The Alchemist

"Annie's knowledge is amazing when it comes to setting a routine, manifesting abundance in all forms and living a wholesome life. I have been following her for almost two years and have completed many of the workshops she has held for the New Moon, Full Moon, visualization and more. Annie The Alchemist helped me become consistent with my daily rituals and I have a beautiful life now with all the work I've done through her guidance."

— Aradhana Arya, Mindset Coach and Yoga Teacher

"Annie The Alchemist is the epitome of presenting yourself as your most authentic self in the modern world. I love her My Little Prayer Book: 75 Prayers, Poems & Mantras for Illumination. It is a perfect anytime reference and self-care-time book to cherish. Her journals also offer inspiration for the every-day."

— Valerie Lunet, Fashion Stylist

"If you're seeking authentic, actionable, and effective practical magic, look no further than Annie Vazquez's guidance, books, and programs. I can say her grounded approach to connecting the dreams and aspirations we have on this planet to the greater transcendence that can transform them into reality has been game changing for me—and I think it will for you, too."

— Shawn Macomber, Editor and Writer

"I have been following Annie The Alchemist since 2021, at a moment in my life that I needed guidance. She has made my spiritual journey so healing and joyous with her workshops, cards, books and guides. So many of my intentions have come to flourish while following Annie's tools. I love that I've been able to incorporate my toddler and boyfriend into the practices since she makes it so easy to follow."

— Karen Castro, Corporate Mama

"Annie The Alchemist's journal prompts always make me dig deeply into the narratives I tell myself and how I can flip that into being authentically present and grateful for every moment of every day."

— Vivian Nosti, Freelance Journalist

More Praise for Annie The Alchemist

"Annie The Alchemist has taught me to dig deep inside and to find the joy in things that I already have and to stay hopeful and positive for my future. Her daily meditation and journal prompts have helped me tremendously."

— Michelle Cocke, Specialized Teacher Assistant

"Annie's meditations and journal prompts have made it easy to continue my daily practice of gratitude. I look forward to her IG Lives and her workshops where I know I can take time for myself and self-reflect."

— Melissa Hago, Beauty & Wellness Trend Forecaster

"I love Annie's Affirmations for Abundance card deck. They are a beautiful way to implement daily inspiration, journaling and self care practices to get your day going and end the day in a positive way. These cards have definitely helped me become peaceful, open up my intuition, and it enforces self care with the journaling."

— Olga Giraldo, Universal Banker & Pro Bollywood Dancer

"Annie Vazquez's My Little Prayer Book: 75 Prayers, Poems & Mantras for Illumination is the best way to be inspired and guided to do great and receive the best. I love Annie and love all the hard work she puts into every single product and meditation she creates."

— Rocio Ruano, Holistic Nutritionist

"Annie does things from the heart. I have been purchasing her workbooks for a while now and I love how detailed her card deck is. I also have My Little Prayer Book: 75 Prayers, Poems & Mantras for Illumination, which has prayers for everything from a Full Moon to a regular Monday."

— Carolina Huerta, Social Services Employee

For my Annie The Alchemist Family.
Thank you all for inspiring this journal and for being beautiful stars, filled with brilliance, love and courageous hearts. Journeying with you all has been one of my greatest adventures.
May we continue to arrive at our destinations, singing and clapping.

"Thank you universe for the *abundance* you bring me today and everyday."

"When you set a *wish* into the universe, you change the *energy* within yourself to make that wish."

Annie the Alchemist's
~~Abundance~~ Journal is for You

Small actions lead to big results. All you need is a few minutes every day with your ABUNDANCE JOURNAL to get the results you wish for.

How The Journal Works:
The Abundance Journal offers you 5 simple prompts. Each one helps to unlock your dreams. The prompts also offer you daily motivation and clarity. All you need to do is fill it out daily to see your wishes come to fruition.

When To Work On Your Journal:
Mornings are the best because they help you set the tone for your day. Then, you can revisit in the evening to see what manifested or what small changes you need to make to get your dreams to arrive.

Results Are Guaranteed:
Journaling is what helped me quit my day job 11 years ago and go after my dreams of writing. It has also been instrumental to hundreds of my students from all over the world. Aside from the 5 daily prompts, I have also included a mix of over 200 original quotes, affirmations, self-care questions, happy tasks, and positive energy tips that I have written throughout the years.

I am so thrilled to see you embark on your journal journey and achieve the results you are looking for.

LOVE AND LIGHT,

Annie Vazquez

My Commitment Page

I, _____ **commit** to journaling daily so I can get the results I am looking for. I know that journaling is a key technique to helping me achieve goals and obtain overall wellness. All I need is a few minutes a day.

I, _____ **commit** to setting the alarm on my phone right now to remind me to journal daily at the same time everyday.

I, _____ **commit** to **ME**.

DATE: / /   MY VISION:_____

_____

_____

SIGNATURE:_____

"*Healing* happens in tiny storms, but like every *Storm*, it passes and the sun comes out."

Instructions:

Follow each prompt and fill out the first 3 in the morning. Then, come back in the evening and fill out the last two prompts.

Today's Intention

(Example) My intention for today is to feel calm, clear, receive good news and finish my project.

Daily Gratitude

(Example) I am grateful for my dog, my exercise, my family and friends.

Self Love Compliment

(Example) I am creative, smart and capable of great things.

favorite Part of Today

(Example) Getting my hair done, seeing my friend, and feeling inner peace. Also, treating myself to chocolate.

Improvement for Tomorrow

(Example) Make time to read book, and check on loved ones.

Today's *Intention*

_____

_____

_____

_____

Daily *Gratitude*

_____

_____

_____

_____

Self *Love* Compliment

_____

_____

_____

_____

favorite Part of Today

_____

_____

_____

_____

Improvement for Tomorrow

_____

_____

_____

_____

7

Today's *Intention*

_____
_____
_____
_____

Daily *Gratitude*

_____
_____
_____
_____

Self *Love* Compliment

_____
_____
_____
_____

favorite Part of Today

_____
_____
_____
_____

Improvement for Tomorrow

_____
_____
_____
_____

Today's *Intention*

_____

_____

_____

_____

Daily *Gratitude*

_____

_____

_____

_____

Self *Love* Compliment

_____

_____

_____

_____

favorite Part of Today

_____

_____

_____

_____

Improvement for Tomorrow

_____

_____

_____

_____

SELF-CARE CHECK IN: What is some
growth, you would like to see for
yourself?

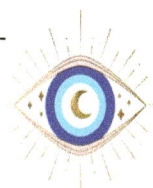

9

DATE: / /

Today's *Intention*

_____
_____
_____
_____

Daily *Gratitude*

_____
_____
_____
_____

Self *Love* Compliment

_____
_____
_____
_____

Favorite Part of Today

_____
_____
_____
_____

Improvement for Tomorrow

_____
_____
_____
_____

10

Today's *Intention*

_____

_____

_____

_____

Daily *Gratitude*

_____

_____

_____

_____

Self *Love* Compliment

_____

_____

_____

_____

favorite Part of Today

_____

_____

_____

_____

Improvement for Tomorrow

_____

_____

_____

_____

Today's *Intention*

_____

_____

_____

_____

Daily *Gratitude*

_____

_____

_____

_____

Self *Love* Compliment

_____

_____

_____

_____

Favorite Part of Today

_____

_____

_____

_____

Improvement for Tomorrow

_____

_____

_____

_____

AFFIRMATION: "There is a divine
team looking after me."

12

"Surrender. *float*.
Respond, don't react.
Let go of the need to
control. Pay *attention*
to situations that
repeat. Observe who
tries to re-enter your
life. Ask yourself:
What am I *learning*?"

How to *Increase* Your Money

1. SPEND IT WITH GRATITUDE.
Pay your bills and say: "thank you for this money."

2. ASK THE UNIVERSE TO HELP YOU CREATE MORE.
Be specific with the amount you desire. You can work with increments and build up over time.

3. BE OPEN TO RECEIVING MONEY.
Say: "I am open to receiving money from all streams possible for me."

4. STAY IN A POSITIVE VIBRATION.
Do things that bring you joy, laughter and love. This raises your vibration and makes you a magnet for money.

Today's *Intention*

_____

_____

_____

_____

Daily *Gratitude*

_____

_____

_____

_____

Self *Love* Compliment

_____

_____

_____

_____

favorite Part of Today

_____

_____

_____

_____

Improvement for Tomorrow

_____

_____

_____

_____

Today's *Intention*

_____
_____
_____
_____

Daily *Gratitude*

_____
_____
_____
_____

Self *Love* **Compliment**

_____
_____
_____
_____

favorite **Part of Today**

_____
_____
_____
_____

Improvement **for Tomorrow**

_____
_____
_____
_____

HAPPY TASK: Write yourself a letter from
your future self 5 years from now.

DATE: / /

Today's *Intention*

_____
_____
_____
_____

Daily *Gratitude*

_____
_____
_____
_____

Self *Love* Compliment

_____
_____
_____
_____

favorite Part of Today

_____
_____
_____
_____

Improvement for Tomorrow

_____
_____
_____
_____

Today's *Intention*

_____
_____
_____
_____

Daily *Gratitude*

_____
_____
_____
_____

Self *Love* Compliment

_____
_____
_____
_____

favorite Part of Today

_____
_____
_____
_____

Improvement for Tomorrow

_____
_____
_____
_____

Today's *Intention*

_____

_____

_____

_____

Daily *Gratitude*

_____

_____

_____

_____

Self *Love* Compliment

_____

_____

_____

_____

favorite Part of Today

_____

_____

_____

_____

Improvement for Tomorrow

_____

_____

_____

_____

QUOTE: "Sometimes, we need to take life one hour at a time."

Today's *Intention*

_____
_____
_____
_____

Daily *Gratitude*

_____
_____
_____
_____

Self *Love* **Compliment**

_____
_____
_____
_____

Favorite **Part of Today**

_____
_____
_____
_____

Improvement **for Tomorrow**

_____
_____
_____
_____

SELF-CARE CHECK IN: Have the daily
self-love compliments helped you
positively shift how you feel about
yourself?

20

Today's *Intention*

_____
_____
_____
_____

Daily *Gratitude*

_____
_____
_____
_____

Self *Love* Compliment

_____
_____
_____
_____

favorite Part of Today

_____
_____
_____
_____

Improvement for Tomorrow

_____
_____
_____
_____

21

I am
Capable

SELF CARE CHECK-IN
What do you need help with today?
Write it down so the universe can help you.

_____

_____

_____

_____

_____

_____

Doodle what's on your mind right now.

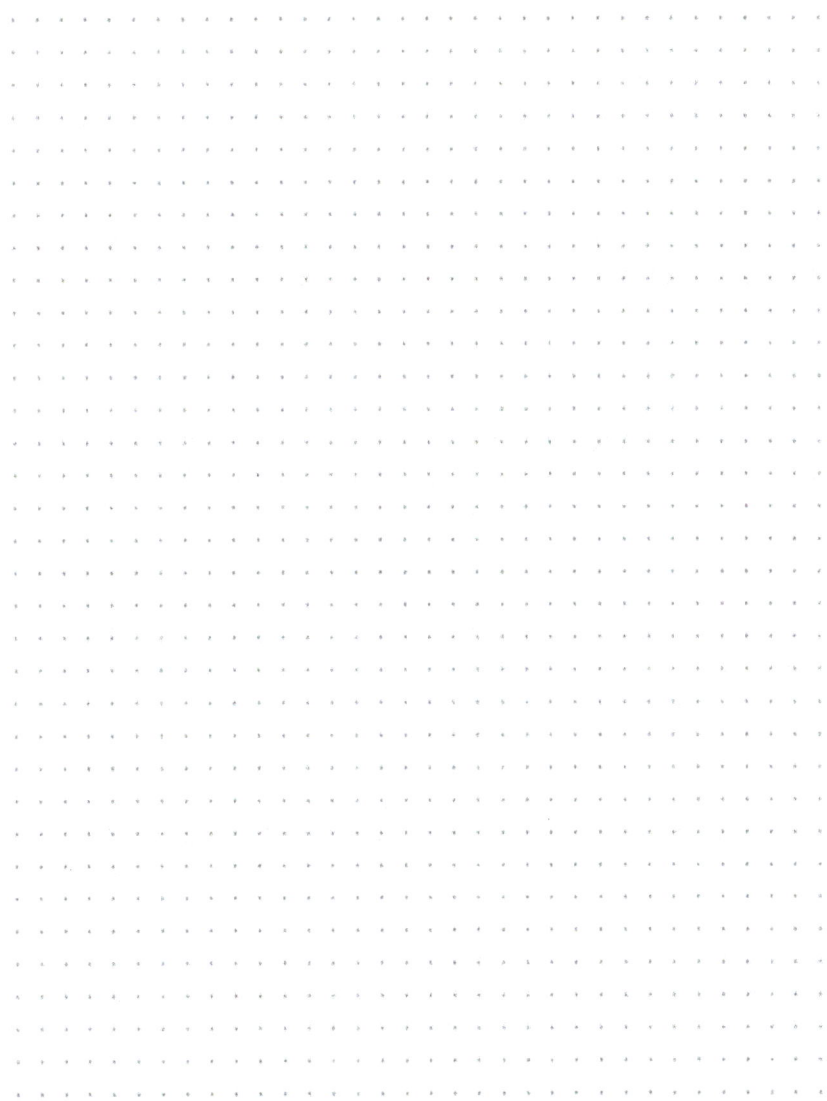

Today's *Intention*

_____
_____
_____
_____

Daily *Gratitude*

_____
_____
_____
_____

Self *Love* **Compliment**

_____
_____
_____
_____

Favorite **Part of Today**

_____
_____
_____
_____

Improvement **for Tomorrow**

_____
_____
_____
_____

Today's *Intention*

_____

_____

_____

_____

Daily *Gratitude*

_____

_____

_____

_____

Self *Love* Compliment

_____

_____

_____

_____

Favorite Part of Today

_____

_____

_____

_____

Improvement for Tomorrow

_____

_____

_____

_____

AFFIRMATION: "I am on a journey,
not a race."

Today's *Intention*

_____
_____
_____
_____

Daily *Gratitude*

_____
_____
_____
_____

Self *Love* Compliment

_____
_____
_____
_____

favorite Part of Today

_____
_____
_____
_____

Improvement for Tomorrow

_____
_____
_____
_____

HAPPY TASK: Place your hands on your
heart and belly to feel calm.

Today's *Intention*

_____
_____
_____
_____

Daily *Gratitude*

_____
_____
_____
_____

Self *Love* Compliment

_____
_____
_____
_____

favorite Part of Today

_____
_____
_____
_____

Improvement for Tomorrow

_____
_____
_____
_____

Today's *Intention*

_____
_____
_____
_____

Daily *Gratitude*

_____
_____
_____
_____

Self *Love* Compliment

_____
_____
_____
_____

Favorite Part of Today

_____
_____
_____
_____

Improvement for Tomorrow

_____
_____
_____
_____

Today's *Intention*

_____

_____

_____

_____

Daily *Gratitude*

_____

_____

_____

_____

Self *Love* Compliment

_____

_____

_____

_____

favorite Part of Today

_____

_____

_____

_____

Improvement for Tomorrow

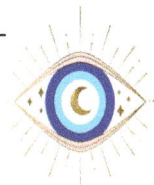

_____

_____

_____

_____

Today's *Intention*

_____

_____

_____

_____

Daily *Gratitude*

_____

_____

_____

_____

Self *Love* Compliment

_____

_____

_____

_____

Favorite Part of Today

_____

_____

_____

_____

Improvement for Tomorrow

_____

_____

_____

_____

28

Today's *Intention*

_____

_____

_____

_____

Daily *Gratitude*

_____

_____

_____

_____

Self *Love* Compliment

_____

_____

_____

_____

favorite Part of Today

_____

_____

_____

_____

Improvement for Tomorrow

_____

_____

_____

_____

Today's *Intention*

_____

_____

_____

_____

Daily *Gratitude*

_____

_____

_____

_____

Self *Love* Compliment

_____

_____

_____

_____

favorite Part of Today

_____

_____

_____

_____

Improvement for Tomorrow

_____

_____

_____

_____

POSITIVE ENERGY TIP: In Feng Shui, water
symbolizes income and abundance. Bringing
in a fountain for your home or office creates
better energy, calms, and refreshes the space.

30

"If the lotus flower can *rise* above the surface to *bloom* in muddy water, remember so can *you*."

Make a List of 100 *Attributes* About Yourself

It may sound like a lot, but there are many amazing things about you. It is important to recognize the beautiful gift you are to this world. You have come this far. Honor yourself with this task.

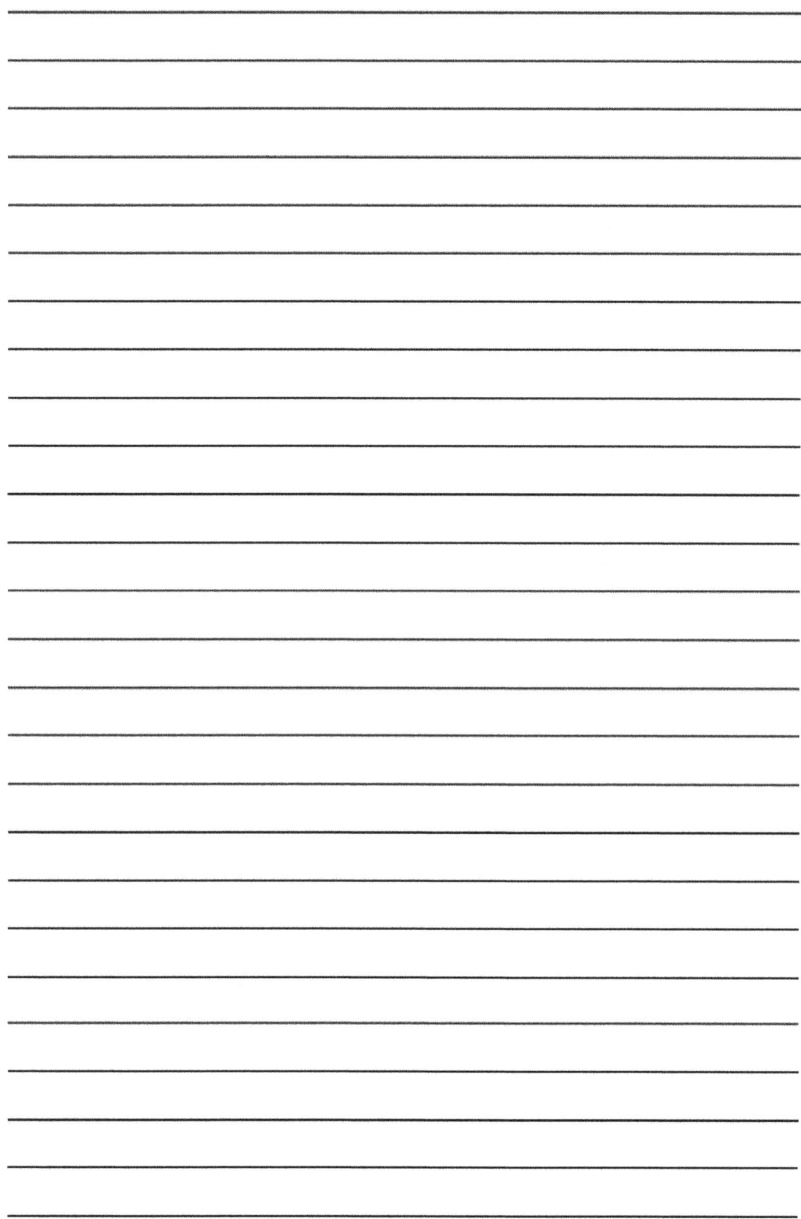

Today's *Intention*

_____
_____
_____
_____

Daily *Gratitude*

_____
_____
_____
_____

Self *Love* Compliment

_____
_____
_____
_____

favorite Part of Today

_____
_____
_____
_____

Improvement for Tomorrow

_____
_____
_____
_____

QUOTE: "Learn to only speak about the
positive in others. If you cannot be positive
about someone else, then just be silent."

34

Today's *Intention*

_____

_____

_____

_____

Daily *Gratitude*

_____

_____

_____

_____

Self *Love* Compliment

_____

_____

_____

_____

favorite Part of Today

_____

_____

_____

_____

Improvement for Tomorrow

_____

_____

_____

_____

Today's *Intention*

_____
_____
_____
_____

Daily *Gratitude*

_____
_____
_____
_____

Self *Love* Compliment

_____
_____
_____
_____

Favorite Part of Today

_____
_____
_____
_____

Improvement for Tomorrow

_____
_____
_____
_____

Today's *Intention*
_____
_____
_____
_____

Daily *Gratitude*
_____
_____
_____
_____

Self *Love* Compliment
_____
_____
_____
_____

favorite Part of Today
_____
_____
_____
_____

Improvement for Tomorrow
_____
_____
_____
_____

SELF-CARE CHECK IN: How do you feel
about your age? What are some great
things about you right now?

Today's *Intention*

_____

_____

_____

_____

Daily *Gratitude*

_____

_____

_____

_____

Self *Love* Compliment

_____

_____

_____

_____

favorite Part of Today

_____

_____

_____

_____

Improvement for Tomorrow

_____

_____

_____

_____

AFFIRMATION: "I am worthy of my
goals and wishes. I know they
will manifest with my effort and faith."

Today's *Intention*

_____
_____
_____
_____

Daily *Gratitude*

_____
_____
_____
_____

Self *Love* Compliment

_____
_____
_____
_____

favorite Part of Today

_____
_____
_____
_____

Improvement for Tomorrow

_____
_____
_____
_____

39

Feng Shui Tip: Internal *Spiritual* Cleanse

1. Pour a glass of water.
2. Squeeze half a lemon in it.
3. Drink it in the morning for the next 7 days.

You will feel re-energized. Water removes toxins, gives you clarity and helps you become more aligned with your goals.

"Sooner or later it will all come together *perfectly* for me."

Today's *Intention*

_____
_____
_____
_____

Daily *Gratitude*

_____
_____
_____
_____

Self *Love* Compliment

_____
_____
_____
_____

favorite Part of Today

_____
_____
_____
_____

Improvement for Tomorrow

_____
_____
_____
_____

HAPPY TASK: Think about 10 years
ago, how have you changed for the
better? List some of your improvements. 42

Today's *Intention*

_____
_____
_____
_____

Daily *Gratitude*

_____
_____
_____
_____

Self *Love* Compliment

_____
_____
_____
_____

Favorite Part of Today

_____
_____
_____
_____

Improvement for Tomorrow

_____
_____
_____
_____

Today's *Intention*

_____

_____

_____

Daily *Gratitude*

_____

_____

_____

Self *Love* Compliment

_____

_____

_____

favorite Part of Today

_____

_____

_____

Improvement for Tomorrow

_____

_____

_____

Today's *Intention*

_____
_____
_____
_____

Daily *Gratitude*

_____
_____
_____
_____

Self *Love* Compliment

_____
_____
_____
_____

favorite Part of Today

_____
_____
_____
_____

Improvement for Tomorrow

_____
_____
_____
_____

HAPPY TASK: List 5 wishes you want
granted this year.

Today's *Intention*

_____
_____
_____
_____

Daily *Gratitude*

_____
_____
_____
_____

Self *Love* Compliment

_____
_____
_____
_____

favorite Part of Today

_____
_____
_____
_____

Improvement for Tomorrow

_____
_____
_____
_____

Today's *Intention*

_____

_____

_____

_____

Daily *Gratitude*

_____

_____

_____

_____

Self *Love* Compliment

_____

_____

_____

_____

favorite Part of Today

_____

_____

_____

_____

Improvement for Tomorrow

_____

_____

_____

_____

Today's *Intention*

_____
_____
_____
_____

Daily *Gratitude*

_____
_____
_____
_____

Self *Love* **Compliment**

_____
_____
_____
_____

Favorite **Part of Today**

_____
_____
_____
_____

Improvement **for Tomorrow**

_____
_____
_____
_____

SELF-CARE CHECK IN:
What is something positive
about yourself you like?

48

"Getting *lost* and taking *detours* is part of the *adventure* of life."

It is *safe* for me to shine.

SELF CARE CHECK-IN

What are some things that help you feel empowered?

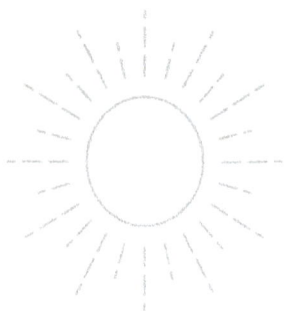

_____

_____

_____

_____

_____

_____

Today's *Intention*

_____

_____

_____

_____

Daily *Gratitude*

_____

_____

_____

_____

Self *Love* Compliment

_____

_____

_____

_____

favorite Part of Today

_____

_____

_____

_____

Improvement for Tomorrow

_____

_____

_____

_____

Today's *Intention*

_____

_____

_____

_____

Daily *Gratitude*

_____

_____

_____

_____

Self *Love* Compliment

_____

_____

_____

_____

Favorite Part of Today

_____

_____

_____

_____

Improvement for Tomorrow

_____

_____

_____

_____

AFFIRMATION: "I also send myself love and light because my soul deserves the same kindness, I give to others."

52

Today's *Intention*

_____
_____
_____
_____

Daily *Gratitude*

_____
_____
_____
_____

Self *Love* Compliment

_____
_____
_____
_____

Favorite Part of Today

_____
_____
_____
_____

Improvement for Tomorrow

_____
_____
_____
_____

DATE: / /

Today's *Intention*

_____
_____
_____
_____

Daily *Gratitude*

_____
_____
_____
_____

Self *Love* Compliment

_____
_____
_____
_____

Favorite Part of Today

_____
_____
_____
_____

Improvement for Tomorrow

_____
_____
_____
_____

54

Today's *Intention*

_____

_____

_____

_____

Daily *Gratitude*

_____

_____

_____

_____

Self *Love* Compliment

_____

_____

_____

_____

Favorite Part of Today

_____

_____

_____

_____

Improvement for Tomorrow

_____

_____

_____

_____

HAPPY TASK: List 5 people you
know and next to their name, write a
positive word that represents them.

55

Today's *Intention*

_____
_____
_____
_____

Daily *Gratitude*

_____
_____
_____
_____

Self *Love* Compliment

_____
_____
_____
_____

favorite Part of Today

_____
_____
_____
_____

Improvement for Tomorrow

_____
_____
_____
_____

QUOTE: "Every journey has a
beginning, middle and end. I accept
all stages to have a good ending."   56

Today's *Intention*

_____

_____

_____

_____

Daily *Gratitude*

_____

_____

_____

_____

Self *Love* Compliment

_____

_____

_____

_____

favorite Part of Today

_____

_____

_____

_____

Improvement for Tomorrow

_____

_____

_____

_____

Express Yourself

"Don't worry about how things will happen. The *universe* has you covered. Just focus on *believing* in the intention."

Today's *Intention*

_____
_____
_____
_____

Daily *Gratitude*

_____
_____
_____
_____

Self *Love* Compliment

_____
_____
_____
_____

Favorite Part of Today

_____
_____
_____
_____

Improvement for Tomorrow

_____
_____
_____
_____

60

Today's *Intention*

_____
_____
_____
_____

Daily *Gratitude*

_____
_____
_____
_____

Self *Love* Compliment

_____
_____
_____
_____

Favorite Part of Today

_____
_____
_____
_____

Improvement for Tomorrow

_____
_____
_____
_____

Today's *Intention*

_____

_____

_____

_____

Daily *Gratitude*

_____

_____

_____

_____

Self *Love* Compliment

_____

_____

_____

_____

favorite Part of Today

_____

_____

_____

_____

Improvement for Tomorrow

_____

_____

_____

_____

Today's *Intention*

_____
_____
_____
_____

Daily *Gratitude*

_____
_____
_____
_____

Self *Love* Compliment

_____
_____
_____
_____

favorite Part of Today

_____
_____
_____
_____

Improvement for Tomorrow

_____
_____
_____
_____

AFFIRMATION: "I am filled with
infinite wisdom."

63

Today's *Intention*

_____

_____

_____

_____

Daily *Gratitude*

_____

_____

_____

_____

Self *Love* Compliment

_____

_____

_____

_____

Favorite Part of Today

_____

_____

_____

_____

Improvement for Tomorrow

_____

_____

_____

_____

Today's *Intention*

_____
_____
_____
_____

Daily *Gratitude*

_____
_____
_____
_____

Self *Love* Compliment

_____
_____
_____
_____

Favorite Part of Today

_____
_____
_____
_____

Improvement for Tomorrow

_____
_____
_____
_____

Today's *Intention*

_____
_____
_____
_____

Daily *Gratitude*

_____
_____
_____
_____

Self *Love* Compliment

_____
_____
_____
_____

Favorite Part of Today

_____
_____
_____
_____

Improvement for Tomorrow

_____
_____
_____

POSITIVE ENERGY TIP: Did you know
peppermint plant, essential oil, and
food can all help you focus better?
Try some today!

66

"Thank you *universe* for removing blocks and clearing the *path* for me."

You are
Strong and *Capable*

Recall a time when things were challenging and
you found the strength to bloom. See how strong and
capable you are. Whenever you feel stuck, remember
this experience to propel you forward.

_____

_____

_____

_____

_____

_____

_____

_____

_____

_____

Today's *Intention*

_____
_____
_____
_____

Daily *Gratitude*

_____
_____
_____
_____

Self *Love* Compliment

_____
_____
_____
_____

favorite Part of Today

_____
_____
_____
_____

Improvement for Tomorrow

_____
_____
_____
_____

QUOTE: "Good news is arriving today
and every day this week."

Today's *Intention*

_____

_____

_____

_____

Daily *Gratitude*

_____

_____

_____

_____

Self *Love* Compliment

_____

_____

_____

_____

Favorite Part of Today

_____

_____

_____

_____

Improvement for Tomorrow

_____

_____

_____

_____

Today's *Intention*

_____
_____
_____
_____

Daily *Gratitude*

_____
_____
_____
_____

Self *Love* Compliment

_____
_____
_____
_____

favorite Part of Today

_____
_____
_____
_____

Improvement for Tomorrow

_____
_____
_____
_____

Today's *Intention*

_____
_____
_____
_____

Daily *Gratitude*

_____
_____
_____
_____

Self *Love* Compliment

_____
_____
_____

favorite Part of Today

_____
_____
_____

Improvement for Tomorrow

_____
_____
_____
_____

SELF-CARE CHECK IN: What is
something, I need to release today
so I can move forward?

72

Today's *Intention*

_____
_____
_____
_____

Daily *Gratitude*

_____
_____
_____
_____

Self *Love* Compliment

_____
_____
_____
_____

Favorite Part of Today

_____
_____
_____
_____

Improvement for Tomorrow

_____
_____
_____
_____

Today's *Intention*

_____
_____
_____
_____

Daily *Gratitude*

_____
_____
_____
_____

Self *Love* Compliment

_____
_____
_____
_____

favorite Part of Today

_____
_____
_____
_____

Improvement for Tomorrow

_____
_____
_____
_____

Today's *Intention*

_____

_____

_____

_____

Daily *Gratitude*

_____

_____

_____

_____

Self *Love* Compliment

_____

_____

_____

_____

favorite Part of Today

_____

_____

_____

_____

Improvement for Tomorrow

_____

_____

_____

_____

AFFIRMATION: "I am proud of
my growth!"

"Anything is *possible* as long as you believe it."

Move to *detox* and shift energy.

The best exercise is the one you enjoy.
Write down ways you love to move.

_____

_____

_____

_____

_____

_____

_____

_____

_____

_____

Today's *Intention*

_____
_____
_____
_____

Daily *Gratitude*

_____
_____
_____
_____

Self *Love* Compliment

_____
_____
_____
_____

favorite Part of Today

_____
_____
_____
_____

Improvement for Tomorrow

_____
_____
_____
_____

HAPPY TASK: Take a mindful shower or bath. Play meditation music, envision the water cleaning off what doesn't serve you and leaving you fresh for new opportunities.

78

Today's *Intention*

_____
_____
_____
_____

Daily *Gratitude*

_____
_____
_____
_____

Self *Love* Compliment

_____
_____
_____
_____

Favorite Part of Today

_____
_____
_____
_____

Improvement for Tomorrow

_____
_____
_____
_____

Today's *Intention*

_____
_____
_____

Daily *Gratitude*

_____
_____
_____
_____

Self *Love* Compliment

_____
_____
_____

favorite Part of Today

_____
_____
_____
_____

Improvement for Tomorrow

_____
_____
_____
_____

Today's *Intention*

_____
_____
_____
_____

Daily *Gratitude*

_____
_____
_____
_____

Self *Love* Compliment

_____
_____
_____
_____

favorite Part of Today

_____
_____
_____
_____

Improvement for Tomorrow

_____
_____
_____
_____

POSITIVE ENERGY TIP: Instead of
saying why is this happening to me,
ask yourself what is this teaching me
about me?

Today's *Intention*

_____
_____
_____
_____

Daily *Gratitude*

_____
_____
_____
_____

Self *Love* Compliment

_____
_____
_____
_____

favorite Part of Today

_____
_____
_____
_____

Improvement for Tomorrow

_____
_____
_____
_____

Today's *Intention*

_____

_____

_____

_____

Daily *Gratitude*

_____

_____

_____

_____

Self *Love* Compliment

_____

_____

_____

_____

favorite Part of Today

_____

_____

_____

_____

Improvement for Tomorrow

_____

_____

_____

_____

Today's *Intention*

_____

_____

_____

_____

Daily *Gratitude*

_____

_____

_____

_____

Self *Love* Compliment

_____

_____

_____

_____

favorite Part of Today

_____

_____

_____

_____

Improvement for Tomorrow

_____

_____

_____

_____

SELF-CARE CHECK IN: Where do I
need to set boundaries?

The universe is *abundant* and there is plenty for everyone.

SELF CARE CHECK-IN
What is something you wish to be abundant in?

_____
_____
_____
_____
_____
_____

Express Yourself

_____
_____
_____
_____
_____
_____
_____
_____
_____
_____
_____
_____
_____
_____
_____
_____
_____
_____
_____
_____
_____
_____
_____
_____
_____

Today's *Intention*

_____
_____
_____
_____

Daily *Gratitude*

_____
_____
_____
_____

Self *Love* Compliment

_____
_____
_____
_____

favorite Part of Today

_____
_____
_____
_____

Improvement for Tomorrow

_____
_____
_____
_____

Today's *Intention*

_____
_____
_____
_____

Daily *Gratitude*

_____
_____
_____
_____

Self *Love* Compliment

_____
_____
_____
_____

Favorite Part of Today

_____
_____
_____
_____

Improvement for Tomorrow

_____
_____
_____
_____

AFFIRMATION: "This week, I will experience 5 things that bring me joy."

88

Today's *Intention*

_____
_____
_____
_____

Daily *Gratitude*

_____
_____
_____
_____

Self *Love* Compliment

_____
_____
_____
_____

favorite Part of Today

_____
_____
_____
_____

Improvement for Tomorrow

_____
_____
_____
_____

Today's *Intention*

_____
_____
_____
_____

Daily *Gratitude*

_____
_____
_____
_____

Self *Love* **Compliment**

_____
_____
_____
_____

favorite **Part of Today**

_____
_____
_____
_____

Improvement **for Tomorrow**

_____
_____
_____
_____

HAPPY TASK: Play binary beats to
improve confidence, motivation, and
calm.

Today's *Intention*

_____
_____
_____
_____

Daily *Gratitude*

_____
_____
_____
_____

Self *Love* Compliment

_____
_____
_____
_____

Favorite Part of Today

_____
_____
_____
_____

Improvement for Tomorrow

_____
_____
_____
_____

Today's *Intention*

_____

_____

_____

_____

Daily *Gratitude*

_____

_____

_____

_____

Self *Love* Compliment

_____

_____

_____

_____

Favorite Part of Today

_____

_____

_____

_____

Improvement for Tomorrow

_____

_____

_____

_____

POSITIVE ENERGY TIP: Angel feathers
are sent to remind you that your
prayers are being answered.

Today's *Intention*

_____

_____

_____

_____

Daily *Gratitude*

_____

_____

_____

_____

Self *Love* Compliment

_____

_____

_____

_____

favorite Part of Today

_____

_____

_____

_____

Improvement for Tomorrow

_____

_____

_____

_____

Doodle what's on your mind right now.

You *deserve* that nap.

Today's *Intention*

_____

_____

_____

_____

Daily *Gratitude*

_____

_____

_____

_____

Self *Love* Compliment

_____

_____

_____

_____

Favorite Part of Today

_____

_____

_____

_____

Improvement for Tomorrow

_____

_____

_____

_____

SELF-CARE CHECK IN: Use
lavender essential oil in your
office space or home to promote
calm energy.

96

Today's *Intention*

_____

_____

_____

_____

Daily *Gratitude*

_____

_____

_____

_____

Self *Love* Compliment

_____

_____

_____

_____

Favorite Part of Today

_____

_____

_____

_____

Improvement for Tomorrow

_____

_____

_____

_____

Today's *Intention*

_____

_____

_____

_____

Daily *Gratitude*

_____

_____

_____

_____

Self *Love* Compliment

_____

_____

_____

_____

favorite Part of Today

_____

_____

_____

_____

Improvement for Tomorrow

_____

_____

_____

_____

DATE: / /

Today's *Intention*

_____
_____
_____

Daily *Gratitude*

_____
_____
_____

Self *Love* Compliment

_____
_____
_____

favorite Part of Today

_____
_____
_____

Improvement for Tomorrow

_____
_____
_____

AFFIRMATION: "I am present for
my presents from the universe."

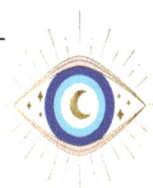

Today's *Intention*

_____
_____
_____
_____

Daily *Gratitude*

_____
_____
_____
_____

Self *Love* Compliment

_____
_____
_____
_____

Favorite Part of Today

_____
_____
_____
_____

Improvement for Tomorrow

_____
_____
_____
_____

Today's *Intention*

_____
_____
_____
_____

Daily *Gratitude*

_____
_____
_____
_____

Self *Love* Compliment

_____
_____
_____
_____

favorite Part of Today

_____
_____
_____
_____

Improvement for Tomorrow

_____
_____
_____
_____

"*Growth* is not a straight line, but a series of squiggly lines going up and down like hills and valleys."

Today's *Intention*

_____
_____
_____
_____

Daily *Gratitude*

_____
_____
_____
_____

Self *Love* Compliment

_____
_____
_____
_____

Favorite Part of Today

_____
_____
_____
_____

Improvement for Tomorrow

_____
_____
_____
_____

Transmuting
Energy

Did you know clapping your hands
together breaks up the negative charges
in the air and turns them to positive energy?

Today's *Intention*

_____

_____

_____

_____

Daily *Gratitude*

_____

_____

_____

_____

Self *Love* Compliment

_____

_____

_____

_____

favorite Part of Today

_____

_____

_____

_____

Improvement for Tomorrow

_____

_____

_____

_____

Today's *Intention*

_____
_____
_____
_____

Daily *Gratitude*

_____
_____
_____
_____

Self *Love* Compliment

_____
_____
_____
_____

favorite Part of Today

_____
_____
_____
_____

Improvement for Tomorrow

_____
_____
_____
_____

POSITIVE ENERGY TIP: In Feng Shui, mirrors represent flow. Place a mirror at your work desk to increase your prosperity.

Today's *Intention*

_____

_____

_____

_____

Daily *Gratitude*

_____

_____

_____

_____

Self *Love* Compliment

_____

_____

_____

_____

favorite Part of Today

_____

_____

_____

_____

Improvement for Tomorrow

_____

_____

_____

_____

Today's *Intention*

_____

_____

_____

_____

Daily *Gratitude*

_____

_____

_____

_____

Self *Love* **Compliment**

_____

_____

_____

_____

Favorite **Part of Today**

_____

_____

_____

_____

Improvement **for Tomorrow**

_____

_____

_____

_____

Today's *Intention*

_____
_____
_____
_____

Daily *Gratitude*

_____
_____
_____
_____

Self *Love* Compliment

_____
_____
_____
_____

favorite Part of Today

_____
_____
_____
_____

Improvement for Tomorrow

_____
_____
_____
_____

QUOTE: "Have no fear, you've got cosmic power."

Today's *Intention*

_____
_____
_____
_____

Daily *Gratitude*

_____
_____
_____
_____

Self *Love* Compliment

_____
_____
_____
_____

favorite Part of Today

_____
_____
_____
_____

Improvement for Tomorrow

_____
_____
_____
_____

SELF-CARE CHECK IN: Did you
know spending time outdoors
cleanses your aura and opens
your 3rd eye?

Today's *Intention*

_____

_____

_____

_____

Daily *Gratitude*

_____

_____

_____

_____

Self *Love* Compliment

_____

_____

_____

_____

favorite Part of Today

_____

_____

_____

_____

Improvement for Tomorrow

_____

_____

_____

_____

POSITIVE ENERGY TIP: 111 is an angel number. Whenever you see it, make a wish.

111

I *choose* not to react, but to respond to life with grace."

SELF-CARE CHECK IN
Where are you ready to welcome expansion in your life?

_____

_____

_____

_____

_____

_____

Express *Yourself*

Today's *Intention*

_____
_____
_____
_____

Daily *Gratitude*

_____
_____
_____
_____

Self *Love* Compliment

_____
_____
_____
_____

Favorite Part of Today

_____
_____
_____
_____

Improvement for Tomorrow

_____
_____
_____
_____

AFFIRMATION: "Everything works
out for me in divine timing."

Today's *Intention*

_____
_____
_____
_____

Daily *Gratitude*

_____
_____
_____
_____

Self *Love* Compliment

_____
_____
_____
_____

favorite Part of Today

_____
_____
_____
_____

Improvement for Tomorrow

_____
_____
_____
_____

Today's *Intention*

_____
_____
_____
_____

Daily *Gratitude*

_____
_____
_____
_____

Self *Love* Compliment

_____
_____
_____
_____

favorite Part of Today

_____
_____
_____
_____

Improvement for Tomorrow

_____
_____
_____
_____

HAPPY TASK: Play ocean waves or
rain recordings tonight to unwind.
Take note of how it soothes
your soul.

Today's *Intention*

_____
_____
_____
_____

Daily *Gratitude*

_____
_____
_____
_____

Self *Love* **Compliment**

_____
_____
_____
_____

favorite **Part of Today**

_____
_____
_____
_____

Improvement **for Tomorrow**

_____
_____
_____
_____

Today's *Intention*

_____
_____
_____
_____

Daily *Gratitude*

_____
_____
_____
_____

Self *Love* **Compliment**

_____
_____
_____
_____

favorite **Part of Today**

_____
_____
_____
_____

Improvement **for Tomorrow**

_____
_____
_____
_____

Today's *Intention*

_____
_____
_____
_____

Daily *Gratitude*

_____
_____
_____
_____

Self *Love* Compliment

_____
_____
_____
_____

Favorite Part of Today

_____
_____
_____
_____

Improvement for Tomorrow

_____
_____
_____
_____

Today's *Intention*

_____
_____
_____
_____

Daily *Gratitude*

_____
_____
_____
_____

Self *Love* Compliment

_____
_____
_____
_____

favorite Part of Today

_____
_____
_____
_____

Improvement for Tomorrow

_____
_____
_____
_____

QUOTE: "Trust that the outcome is
in your favor."

Write down 10 things you want to manifest in your life now.

_____

_____

_____

_____

_____

_____

_____

_____

_____

_____

_____

_____

_____

_____

_____

_____

_____

_____

_____

_____

"You are *energy* and therefore you must recharge."

Today's *Intention*

_____
_____
_____
_____

Daily *Gratitude*

_____
_____
_____
_____

Self *Love* Compliment

_____
_____
_____
_____

favorite Part of Today

_____
_____
_____
_____

Improvement for Tomorrow

_____
_____
_____
_____

Today's *Intention*

_____
_____
_____
_____

Daily *Gratitude*

_____
_____
_____
_____

Self *Love* Compliment

_____
_____
_____
_____

Favorite Part of Today

_____
_____
_____
_____

Improvement for Tomorrow

_____
_____
_____
_____

HAPPY TASK: Watch the sunrise.

124

Today's *Intention*

_____
_____
_____
_____

Daily *Gratitude*

_____
_____
_____
_____

Self *Love* Compliment

_____
_____
_____
_____

favorite Part of Today

_____
_____
_____
_____

Improvement for Tomorrow

_____
_____
_____
_____

Today's *Intention*

_____

_____

_____

_____

Daily *Gratitude*

_____

_____

_____

_____

Self *Love* Compliment

_____

_____

_____

_____

favorite Part of Today

_____

_____

_____

_____

Improvement for Tomorrow

_____

_____

_____

_____

AFFIRMATION: "I am lovable."

Today's *Intention*

_____

_____

_____

_____

Daily *Gratitude*

_____

_____

_____

_____

Self *Love* Compliment

_____

_____

_____

_____

Favorite Part of Today

_____

_____

_____

_____

Improvement for Tomorrow

_____

_____

_____

_____

Today's *Intention*

_____

_____

_____

_____

Daily *Gratitude*

_____

_____

_____

_____

Self *Love* Compliment

_____

_____

_____

_____

favorite Part of Today

_____

_____

_____

_____

Improvement for Tomorrow

_____

_____

_____

_____

HAPPY TASK: This evening, shut off
electronics an hour before going to sleep.
Instead, read positive quotes, a good book,
or journal. Compare the experience.

Today's *Intention*

_____

_____

_____

_____

Daily *Gratitude*

_____

_____

_____

_____

Self *Love* Compliment

_____

_____

_____

_____

favorite Part of Today

_____

_____

_____

_____

Improvement for Tomorrow

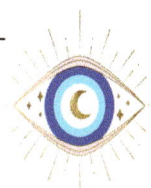

_____

_____

_____

_____

5 Simple *Steps* to Problem Solving

1. Sit quietly with the issue.
2. Ask yourself: "What is this teaching me?"
3. Thank the universe for helping you grow.
4. Write 3 ways to resolve the issue on paper.
5. Light a candle and say: "This problem is now resolved. I ask the universe for courage and enlightenment as I move forward.

"*Intentions*
work when
they are
backed up by
actions."

Today's *Intention*

_____

_____

_____

_____

Daily *Gratitude*

_____

_____

_____

_____

Self *Love* Compliment

_____

_____

_____

_____

favorite Part of Today

_____

_____

_____

_____

Improvement for Tomorrow

_____

_____

_____

_____

POSITIVE ENERGY TIP: Rub your belly
to activate your strength and inner
confidence. (Solar plexus chakra)

Today's *Intention*

_____

_____

_____

_____

Daily *Gratitude*

_____

_____

_____

_____

Self *Love* **Compliment**

_____

_____

_____

_____

favorite **Part of Today**

_____

_____

_____

_____

Improvement **for Tomorrow**

_____

_____

_____

_____

Today's *Intention*

_____

_____

_____

_____

Daily *Gratitude*

_____

_____

_____

_____

Self *Love* Compliment

_____

_____

_____

_____

favorite Part of Today

_____

_____

_____

_____

Improvement for Tomorrow

_____

_____

_____

_____

Today's *Intention*

_____

_____

_____

_____

Daily *Gratitude*

_____

_____

_____

_____

Self *Love* Compliment

_____

_____

_____

_____

Favorite Part of Today

_____

_____

_____

_____

Improvement for Tomorrow

_____

_____

_____

_____

AFFIRMATION: "When things get tough, it's because I am about to have a miracle breakthrough."

Today's *Intention*

_____
_____
_____
_____

Daily *Gratitude*

_____
_____
_____
_____

Self *Love* Compliment

_____
_____
_____
_____

favorite Part of Today

_____
_____
_____
_____

Improvement for Tomorrow

_____
_____
_____
_____

Today's *Intention*

_____
_____
_____
_____

Daily *Gratitude*

_____
_____
_____
_____

Self *Love* Compliment

_____
_____
_____
_____

Favorite Part of Today

_____
_____
_____
_____

Improvement for Tomorrow

_____
_____
_____
_____

Today's *Intention*

_____

_____

_____

_____

Daily *Gratitude*

_____

_____

_____

_____

Self *Love* Compliment

_____

_____

_____

_____

favorite Part of Today

_____

_____

_____

_____

Improvement for Tomorrow

_____

_____

_____

_____

AFFIRMATION: "I forgive others
and it opens doors to new
opportunities."

138

"Everyone *expresses* love differently."

We are all works in *progress*

SELF CARE CHECK-IN

Is there someone you need to forgive? Forgiveness automatically removes blocks from your life and creates positive abundance. Make a list of who you need to forgive and next to their name write: "I forgive you and I set myself free." Get ready for good things to happen!

_____

_____

_____

_____

_____

Today's *Intention*

_____
_____
_____
_____

Daily *Gratitude*

_____
_____
_____
_____

Self *Love* Compliment

_____
_____
_____
_____

favorite Part of Today

_____
_____
_____
_____

Improvement for Tomorrow

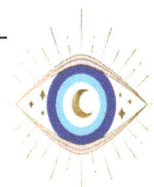

_____
_____
_____
_____

Today's *Intention*

_____

_____

_____

_____

Daily *Gratitude*

_____

_____

_____

_____

Self *Love* Compliment

_____

_____

_____

_____

favorite Part of Today

_____

_____

_____

_____

Improvement for Tomorrow

_____

_____

_____

_____

HAPPY TASK: Doing something new aids in
removing blocks, strengthens our mind, and
helps us see our infinite courage. What is
something new you can do today?

142

Today's *Intention*

Daily *Gratitude*

Self *Love* Compliment

---

favorite Part of Today

Improvement for Tomorrow

Today's *Intention*

_____

_____

_____

_____

Daily *Gratitude*

_____

_____

_____

_____

Self *Love* Compliment

_____

_____

_____

_____

Favorite Part of Today

_____

_____

_____

_____

Improvement for Tomorrow

_____

_____

_____

_____

POSITIVE ENERGY TIP: Being
vulnerable allows people to feel
closer to you and helps you build
beautiful caring bonds with others.

144

Today's *Intention*

_____
_____
_____
_____

Daily *Gratitude*

_____
_____
_____
_____

Self *Love* **Compliment**

_____
_____
_____
_____

favorite **Part of Today**

_____
_____
_____
_____

Improvement **for Tomorrow**

_____
_____
_____
_____

Today's *Intention*

_____
_____
_____
_____

Daily *Gratitude*

_____
_____
_____
_____

Self *Love* Compliment

_____
_____
_____
_____

favorite Part of Today

_____
_____
_____
_____

Improvement for Tomorrow

_____
_____
_____
_____

SELF-CARE CHECK IN: How does
the energy of your space feel?

146

Today's *Intention*

_____

_____

_____

_____

Daily *Gratitude*

_____

_____

_____

_____

Self *Love* **Compliment**

_____

_____

_____

_____

favorite **Part of Today**

_____

_____

_____

_____

Improvement **for Tomorrow**

_____

_____

_____

_____

When I tap into my inner child, the adult in me *flourishes*.

Create a playlist of good vibes music that you can always turn to when you need a positive energy boost.

_____

_____

_____

_____

_____

_____

_____

_____

_____

_____

"The love
I give
is my
karma."

Today's *Intention*

_____
_____
_____
_____

Daily *Gratitude*

_____
_____
_____
_____

Self *Love* Compliment

_____
_____
_____
_____

Favorite Part of Today

_____
_____
_____
_____

Improvement for Tomorrow

_____
_____
_____
_____

AFFIRMATION:
"I am self-motivated."

Today's *Intention*

_____

_____

_____

_____

Daily *Gratitude*

_____

_____

_____

_____

Self *Love* Compliment

_____

_____

_____

_____

favorite Part of Today

_____

_____

_____

_____

Improvement for Tomorrow

_____

_____

_____

_____

Today's *Intention*

_____

_____

_____

_____

Daily *Gratitude*

_____

_____

_____

_____

Self *Love* Compliment

_____

_____

_____

_____

favorite Part of Today

_____

_____

_____

_____

Improvement for Tomorrow

_____

_____

_____

_____

HAPPY TASK: Light a candle for your
ancestors today and ask them to guide
you on something you need help with.   152

Today's *Intention*

_____

_____

_____

_____

Daily *Gratitude*

_____

_____

_____

_____

Self *Love* Compliment

_____

_____

_____

_____

Favorite Part of Today

_____

_____

_____

_____

Improvement for Tomorrow

_____

_____

_____

_____

Today's *Intention*

_____

_____

_____

_____

Daily *Gratitude*

_____

_____

_____

_____

Self *Love* **Compliment**

_____

_____

_____

_____

favorite **Part of Today**

_____

_____

_____

_____

Improvement **for Tomorrow**

_____

_____

_____

_____

Today's *Intention*

_____

_____

_____

_____

Daily *Gratitude*

_____

_____

_____

_____

Self *Love* Compliment

_____

_____

_____

_____

favorite Part of Today

_____

_____

_____

_____

Improvement for Tomorrow

_____

_____

_____

_____

Today's *Intention*

_____

_____

_____

_____

Daily *Gratitude*

_____

_____

_____

_____

Self *Love* **Compliment**

_____

_____

_____

_____

favorite **Part of Today**

_____

_____

_____

_____

Improvement **for Tomorrow**

_____

_____

_____

_____

QUOTE: "To win, I have to risk loss and
I'm willing to take the risk on myself."

"The universe *speaks* in codes: signs, numbers, repeating *conversations*, and animal totems."

Clear out the old

What are some things you are no longer using that you can let go of now to create more space to receive abundance?

☐ _____   ☐ _____

☐ _____   ☐ _____

☐ _____   ☐ _____

☐ _____   ☐ _____

☐ _____   ☐ _____

☐ _____   ☐ _____

Today's *Intention*

_____

_____

_____

_____

Daily *Gratitude*

_____

_____

_____

_____

Self *Love* **Compliment**

_____

_____

_____

_____

favorite **Part of Today**

_____

_____

_____

_____

Improvement **for Tomorrow**

_____

_____

_____

_____

Today's *Intention*

Daily *Gratitude*

Self *Love* Compliment

---

favorite Part of Today

Improvement for Tomorrow

SELF-CARE CHECK IN: Do you take
mindful breaks throughout the day to
get fresh air, stretch, and breathe?   160

Today's *Intention*

_____

_____

_____

_____

Daily *Gratitude*

_____

_____

_____

_____

Self *Love* Compliment

_____

_____

_____

_____

favorite Part of Today

_____

_____

_____

_____

Improvement for Tomorrow

_____

_____

_____

_____

Today's *Intention*

_____

_____

_____

_____

Daily *Gratitude*

_____

_____

_____

_____

Self *Love* **Compliment**

_____

_____

_____

_____

favorite **Part of Today**

_____

_____

_____

_____

Improvement **for Tomorrow**

_____

_____

_____

_____

AFFIRMATION: "My creativity
flows beautifully like the ocean."

Today's *Intention*

_____
_____
_____
_____

Daily *Gratitude*

_____
_____
_____
_____

Self *Love* **Compliment**

_____
_____
_____
_____

favorite **Part of Today**

_____
_____
_____
_____

Improvement **for Tomorrow**

_____
_____
_____
_____

Today's *Intention*

_____

_____

_____

_____

Daily *Gratitude*

_____

_____

_____

_____

Self *Love* Compliment

_____

_____

_____

_____

favorite Part of Today

_____

_____

_____

_____

Improvement for Tomorrow

_____

_____

_____

_____

AFFIRMATION: "I feel healthy,
grounded and strong in my body."

Today's *Intention*

_____

_____

_____

_____

Daily *Gratitude*

_____

_____

_____

_____

Self *Love* **Compliment**

_____

_____

_____

_____

favorite **Part of Today**

_____

_____

_____

_____

Improvement **for Tomorrow**

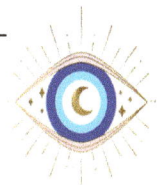

_____

_____

_____

_____

Doodle what's on your mind right now.

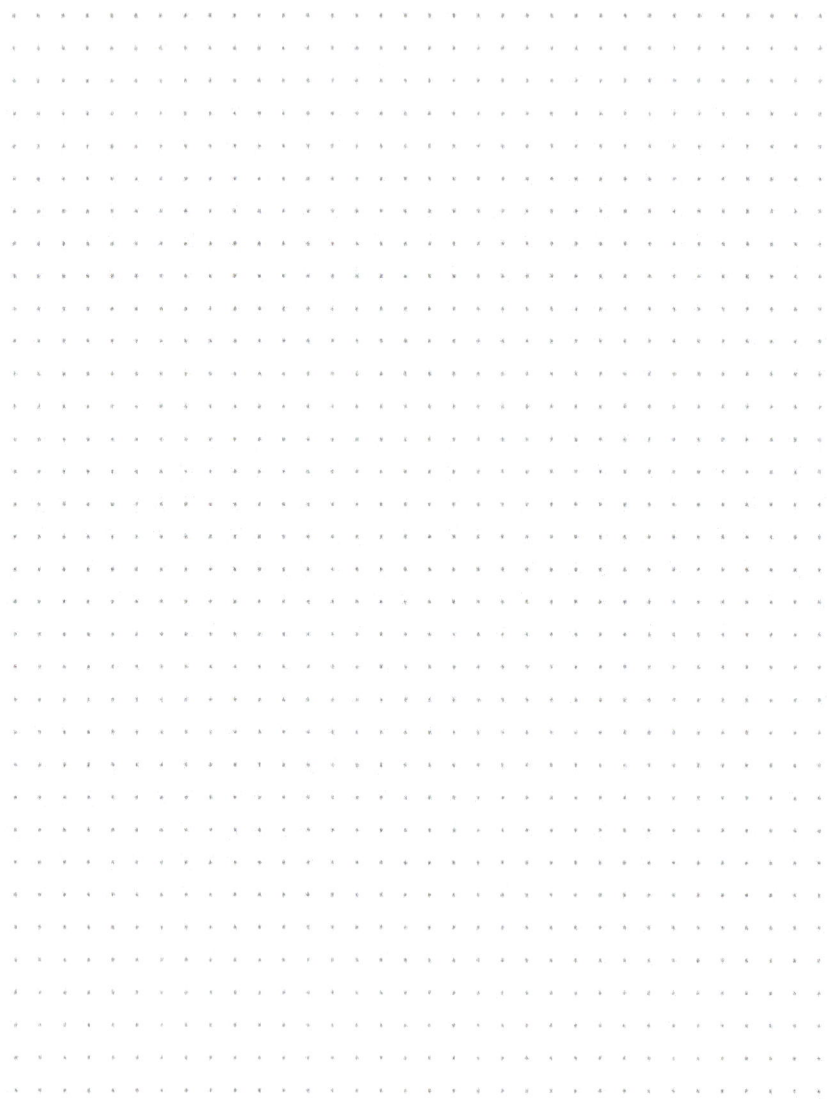

"The only person that stands in my way is *me*. Therefore, I move out of my way and *surrender* to the universe to help me on my path."

Today's *Intention*

_____

_____

_____

_____

Daily *Gratitude*

_____

_____

_____

_____

Self *Love* Compliment

_____

_____

_____

_____

favorite Part of Today

_____

_____

_____

_____

Improvement for Tomorrow

_____

_____

_____

_____

POSITIVE ENERGY TIP: Sprinkling
lavender oil on bedsheets and pillow
cases helps to calm and bring a good 168
night's rest.

Today's *Intention*

_____
_____
_____
_____

Daily *Gratitude*

_____
_____
_____
_____

Self *Love* Compliment

_____
_____
_____
_____

Favorite Part of Today

_____
_____
_____
_____

Improvement for Tomorrow

_____
_____
_____
_____

Today's *Intention*

_____

_____

_____

_____

Daily *Gratitude*

_____

_____

_____

_____

Self *Love* Compliment

_____

_____

_____

_____

favorite Part of Today

_____

_____

_____

_____

Improvement for Tomorrow

_____

_____

_____

_____

AFFIRMATION: "I am intuitive, clear
and I flow in the right direction."
170

Today's *Intention*

_____
_____
_____

Daily *Gratitude*

_____
_____
_____
_____

Self *Love* Compliment

_____
_____
_____
_____

favorite Part of Today

_____
_____
_____
_____

Improvement for Tomorrow

_____
_____
_____
_____

Today's *Intention*

_____

_____

_____

_____

Daily *Gratitude*

_____

_____

_____

_____

Self *Love* **Compliment**

_____

_____

_____

_____

favorite **Part of Today**

_____

_____

_____

_____

Improvement **for Tomorrow**

_____

_____

_____

_____

Today's *Intention*

_____

_____

_____

_____

Daily *Gratitude*

_____

_____

_____

_____

Self *Love* Compliment

_____

_____

_____

_____

favorite Part of Today

_____

_____

_____

_____

Improvement for Tomorrow

_____

_____

_____

_____

Today's *Intention*

_____
_____
_____
_____

Daily *Gratitude*

_____
_____
_____
_____

Self *Love* **Compliment**

_____
_____
_____
_____

Favorite **Part of Today**

_____
_____
_____
_____

Improvement **for Tomorrow**

_____
_____
_____
_____

AFFIRMATION: "I surrender to the
universe and I open myself to receive
the abundance it has for me today." 174

"Pain exists but so does *love*. Everything is *yin-yang*."

If I *fail*, I simply get up and start over. It is that *simple*.

SELF CARE CHECK-IN

When was the last time you were willing to be bad at something in order to learn and become good at it later?

_____

_____

_____

_____

_____

_____

Today's *Intention*

_____

_____

_____

_____

Daily *Gratitude*

_____

_____

_____

_____

Self *Love* Compliment

_____

_____

_____

_____

favorite Part of Today

_____

_____

_____

_____

Improvement for Tomorrow

_____

_____

_____

_____

Today's *Intention*

_____

_____

_____

_____

Daily *Gratitude*

_____

_____

_____

_____

Self *Love* Compliment

_____

_____

_____

_____

Favorite Part of Today

_____

_____

_____

_____

Improvement for Tomorrow

_____

_____

_____

_____

HAPPY TASK: Write about someone you can be
vulnerable and comfortable with. If you don't
have someone, imagine what they would be
like and manifest them into your life.

178

Today's *Intention*

Daily *Gratitude*

Self *Love* Compliment

---

favorite Part of Today

Improvement for Tomorrow

Today's *Intention*

_____

_____

_____

_____

Daily *Gratitude*

_____

_____

_____

_____

Self *Love* Compliment

_____

_____

_____

_____

favorite Part of Today

_____

_____

_____

_____

Improvement for Tomorrow

_____

_____

_____

_____

AFFIRMATION: "I am ready to enter
a new chapter in my life that is filled
with miracles."

Today's *Intention*

_____

_____

_____

_____

Daily *Gratitude*

_____

_____

_____

_____

Self *Love* Compliment

_____

_____

_____

_____

Favorite Part of Today

_____

_____

_____

_____

Improvement for Tomorrow

_____

_____

_____

_____

Today's *Intention*

_____

_____

_____

_____

Daily *Gratitude*

_____

_____

_____

_____

Self *Love* Compliment

_____

_____

_____

_____

favorite Part of Today

_____

_____

_____

_____

Improvement for Tomorrow

_____

_____

_____

_____

QUOTE: "Angel numbers like 111, 222,
333 are your angels reminding you
they have your back."

Today's *Intention*

_____
_____
_____
_____

Daily *Gratitude*

_____
_____
_____
_____

Self *Love* Compliment

_____
_____
_____
_____

favorite Part of Today

_____
_____
_____
_____

Improvement for Tomorrow

_____
_____
_____
_____

Make a list of compliments that praise you for your character and not your physical appearance. Use some this week.

_____

_____

_____

_____

_____

_____

_____

_____

_____

_____

_____

_____

_____

_____

_____

_____

_____

_____

_____

_____

_____

_____

"Everyone is on *different* parts of the journey. Therefore, I don't compare *myself* to anyone."

Today's *Intention*

_____
_____
_____
_____

Daily *Gratitude*

_____
_____
_____
_____

Self *Love* Compliment

_____
_____
_____
_____

favorite Part of Today

_____
_____
_____
_____

Improvement for Tomorrow

_____
_____
_____
_____

QUOTE: "Our vibes speak louder than our words."

Today's *Intention*

_____
_____
_____
_____

Daily *Gratitude*

_____
_____
_____
_____

Self *Love* Compliment

_____
_____
_____
_____

Favorite Part of Today

_____
_____
_____
_____

Improvement for Tomorrow

_____
_____
_____
_____

Today's *Intention*

_____

_____

_____

Daily *Gratitude*

_____

_____

_____

_____

Self *Love* Compliment

_____

_____

_____

Favorite Part of Today

_____

_____

_____

_____

Improvement for Tomorrow

_____

_____

_____

_____

Today's *Intention*

_____

_____

_____

Daily *Gratitude*

_____

_____

_____

Self *Love* Compliment

_____

_____

_____

favorite Part of Today

_____

_____

_____

Improvement for Tomorrow

_____

_____

_____

_____

AFFIRMATION: "I am a great problem solver."

Today's *Intention*

_____
_____
_____
_____

Daily *Gratitude*

_____
_____
_____
_____

Self *Love* Compliment

_____
_____
_____
_____

Favorite Part of Today

_____
_____
_____
_____

Improvement for Tomorrow

_____
_____
_____
_____

Today's *Intention*

_____

_____

_____

_____

Daily *Gratitude*

_____

_____

_____

_____

Self *Love* Compliment

_____

_____

_____

_____

Favorite Part of Today

_____

_____

_____

_____

Improvement for Tomorrow

_____

_____

_____

_____

Today's *Intention*

_____
_____
_____
_____

Daily *Gratitude*

_____
_____
_____
_____

Self *Love* Compliment

_____
_____
_____
_____

Favorite Part of Today

_____
_____
_____
_____

Improvement for Tomorrow

_____
_____
_____
_____

HAPPY TASK: Walk barefoot on the
grass for grounding.

"My calendar
is booked
with *blessings*,
celebrations and
lots of *love*."

Washing *Stagnant* Energy

Water is known for washing off stagnant energy and recalibrating our good vibes. What ways do you like to cleanse stagnant energy?

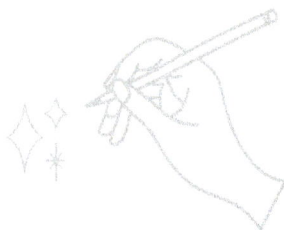

_____

_____

_____

_____

_____

_____

_____

_____

_____

_____

Today's *Intention*

_____
_____
_____
_____

Daily *Gratitude*

_____
_____
_____
_____

Self *Love* Compliment

_____
_____
_____
_____

favorite Part of Today

_____
_____
_____
_____

Improvement for Tomorrow

_____
_____
_____
_____

Today's *Intention*

_____

_____

_____

_____

Daily *Gratitude*

_____

_____

_____

_____

Self *Love* **Compliment**

_____

_____

_____

_____

Favorite **Part of Today**

_____

_____

_____

_____

Improvement **for Tomorrow**

_____

_____

_____

_____

AFFRIMATION: "I am grateful to be
surrounded by loving and loyal
people."

196

DATE: / /

Today's *Intention*

_____
_____
_____
_____

Daily *Gratitude*

_____
_____
_____
_____

Self *Love* Compliment

_____
_____
_____
_____

favorite Part of Today

_____
_____
_____
_____

Improvement for Tomorrow

_____
_____
_____
_____

Today's *Intention*

_____
_____
_____
_____

Daily *Gratitude*

_____
_____
_____
_____

Self *Love* Compliment

_____
_____
_____
_____

Favorite Part of Today

_____
_____
_____
_____

Improvement for Tomorrow

_____
_____
_____
_____

AFFIRMATION: "I don't spend time,
I invest in it."

Today's *Intention*

_____
_____
_____
_____

Daily *Gratitude*

_____
_____
_____
_____

Self *Love* Compliment

_____
_____
_____
_____

Favorite Part of Today

_____
_____
_____
_____

Improvement for Tomorrow

_____
_____
_____
_____

Today's *Intention*

_____

_____

_____

_____

Daily *Gratitude*

_____

_____

_____

_____

Self *Love* Compliment

_____

_____

_____

_____

favorite Part of Today

_____

_____

_____

_____

Improvement for Tomorrow

_____

_____

_____

_____

QUOTE: "Measure your life by all the
things you have to be grateful for."

200

Today's *Intention*

_____
_____
_____
_____

Daily *Gratitude*

_____
_____
_____
_____

Self *Love* Compliment

_____
_____
_____
_____

favorite Part of Today

_____
_____
_____
_____

Improvement for Tomorrow

_____
_____
_____
_____

I have *peace* with my past.

SELF CARE CHECK-IN

Write a letter to someone you need to forgive. This action will clear you of blocked energy and open the door to your blessings.

_____
_____
_____
_____
_____
_____
_____
_____
_____

"Have more *fun*. This is all *Temporary*."

Today's *Intention*

_____

_____

_____

_____

Daily *Gratitude*

_____

_____

_____

_____

Self *Love* Compliment

_____

_____

_____

favorite Part of Today

_____

_____

_____

Improvement for Tomorrow

_____

_____

_____

HAPPY TASK: Clear your throat chakra
to manifest easier by singing or
drinking lemon water.

Today's *Intention*

_____
_____
_____
_____

Daily *Gratitude*

_____
_____
_____
_____

Self *Love* Compliment

_____
_____
_____
_____

favorite Part of Today

_____
_____
_____
_____

Improvement for Tomorrow

_____
_____
_____
_____

Today's *Intention*

_____
_____
_____

Daily *Gratitude*

_____
_____
_____
_____

Self *Love* Compliment

_____
_____
_____

favorite Part of Today

_____
_____
_____

Improvement for Tomorrow

_____
_____
_____
_____

Today's *Intention*

_____

_____

_____

_____

Daily *Gratitude*

_____

_____

_____

_____

Self *Love* Compliment

_____

_____

_____

_____

favorite Part of Today

_____

_____

_____

_____

Improvement for Tomorrow

_____

_____

_____

_____

AFFIRMATION: "When I cleanse
my physical space, I also cleanse
my soul."

Today's *Intention*

_____

_____

_____

_____

Daily *Gratitude*

_____

_____

_____

_____

Self *Love* **Compliment**

_____

_____

_____

_____

Favorite **Part of Today**

_____

_____

_____

_____

Improvement **for Tomorrow**

_____

_____

_____

_____

Today's *Intention*

_____
_____
_____
_____

Daily *Gratitude*

_____
_____
_____
_____

Self *Love* Compliment

_____
_____
_____
_____

favorite Part of Today

_____
_____
_____
_____

Improvement for Tomorrow

_____
_____
_____
_____

Today's *Intention*

_____
_____
_____
_____

Daily *Gratitude*

_____
_____
_____
_____

Self *Love* **Compliment**

_____
_____
_____
_____

favorite **Part of Today**

_____
_____
_____
_____

Improvement **for Tomorrow**

_____
_____
_____
_____

HAPPY TASK: Compliment a stranger.

"The *real* glow up happens when you *heal* yourself from the inside."

Think of a time when you felt divine guidance. What was it like?

_____

_____

_____

_____

_____

_____

_____

_____

_____

_____

_____

_____

_____

_____

_____

_____

_____

_____

_____

_____

_____

Today's *Intention*

Daily *Gratitude*

Self *Love* Compliment

---

favorite Part of Today

Improvement for Tomorrow

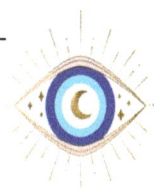

Today's *Intention*

_____

_____

_____

_____

Daily *Gratitude*

_____

_____

_____

_____

Self *Love* **Compliment**

_____

_____

_____

_____

favorite **Part of Today**

_____

_____

_____

_____

Improvement **for Tomorrow**

_____

_____

_____

_____

HAPPY TASK: Tell someone how grateful you are to have them in your life.

214

Today's *Intention*

_____
_____
_____
_____

Daily *Gratitude*

_____
_____
_____
_____

Self *Love* Compliment

_____
_____
_____
_____

favorite Part of Today

_____
_____
_____
_____

Improvement for Tomorrow

_____
_____
_____
_____

Today's *Intention*

_____

_____

_____

_____

Daily *Gratitude*

_____

_____

_____

_____

Self *Love* **Compliment**

_____

_____

_____

_____

Favorite **Part of Today**

_____

_____

_____

_____

Improvement **for Tomorrow**

_____

_____

_____

_____

AFFIRMATION: "My goals are achievable!"

216

Today's *Intention*

_____
_____
_____
_____

Daily *Gratitude*

_____
_____
_____
_____

Self *Love* Compliment

_____
_____
_____
_____

favorite Part of Today

_____
_____
_____
_____

Improvement for Tomorrow

_____
_____
_____
_____

217

Today's *Intention*

_____
_____
_____
_____

Daily *Gratitude*

_____
_____
_____
_____

Self *Love* **Compliment**

_____
_____
_____
_____

Favorite **Part of Today**

_____
_____
_____
_____

Improvement **for Tomorrow**

_____
_____
_____
_____

QUOTE: "She was not afraid to show her heart's scars for she knew each wound symbolized all the times she gave it her best shot."

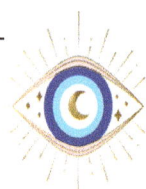

218

Today's *Intention*

_____
_____
_____
_____

Daily *Gratitude*

_____
_____
_____
_____

Self *Love* Compliment

_____
_____
_____
_____

favorite Part of Today

_____
_____
_____
_____

Improvement for Tomorrow

_____
_____
_____
_____

Water is *Life!*

Reach for water instead of coffee when you need more energy throughout the day. Staying hydrated with water helps you feel and flow better.

☐ 8am - 10am *Morning*

☐ 12pm - 2pm *Lunch*

☐ 4pm - 6pm *Evening*

☐ 1 big glass 2 hours before bed

"If you want to make *waves* in this life, you will have to start by making *ripples* first."

Today's *Intention*

_____
_____
_____
_____

Daily *Gratitude*

_____
_____
_____
_____

Self *Love* Compliment

_____
_____
_____
_____

favorite Part of Today

_____
_____
_____
_____

Improvement for Tomorrow

_____
_____
_____
_____

AFFIRMATION: "I release relationships
that no longer serve me and I attract
new ones that are aligned with my
beliefs."

222

Today's *Intention*

_____
_____
_____
_____

Daily *Gratitude*

_____
_____
_____
_____

Self *Love* **Compliment**

_____
_____
_____
_____

favorite **Part of Today**

_____
_____
_____
_____

Improvement **for Tomorrow**

_____
_____
_____
_____

223

Today's *Intention*

_____

_____

_____

_____

Daily *Gratitude*

_____

_____

_____

_____

Self *Love* Compliment

_____

_____

_____

_____

favorite Part of Today

_____

_____

_____

_____

Improvement for Tomorrow

_____

_____

_____

_____

Today's *Intention*

_____
_____
_____

Daily *Gratitude*

_____
_____
_____

Self *Love* Compliment

_____
_____
_____

favorite Part of Today

_____
_____
_____

Improvement for Tomorrow

_____
_____
_____

AFFIRMATION: "Every time I do
something nice for myself, the universe
rewards me with more nice things."

225

Today's *Intention*

_____

_____

_____

_____

Daily *Gratitude*

_____

_____

_____

_____

Self *Love* Compliment

_____

_____

_____

_____

Favorite Part of Today

_____

_____

_____

_____

Improvement for Tomorrow

_____

_____

_____

_____

Today's *Intention*

_____

_____

_____

_____

Daily *Gratitude*

_____

_____

_____

_____

Self *Love* Compliment

_____

_____

_____

_____

favorite Part of Today

_____

_____

_____

_____

Improvement for Tomorrow

_____

_____

_____

_____

Today's *Intention*

_____
_____
_____
_____

Daily *Gratitude*

_____
_____
_____
_____

Self *Love* Compliment

_____
_____
_____
_____

favorite Part of Today

_____
_____
_____
_____

Improvement for Tomorrow

_____
_____
_____
_____

AFFIRMATION: "I trust my intuition."

"I am *no* longer letting anyone turn on my energy faucet and *drain* me."

Everyone is *growing* through something. Be kind.

SELF CARE CHECK-IN

What is your current dream and how are you nurturing your soul as you work on it?

_____

_____

_____

_____

_____

_____

_____

_____

_____

_____

_____

_____

Today's *Intention*

_____

_____

_____

_____

Daily *Gratitude*

_____

_____

_____

_____

Self *Love* Compliment

_____

_____

_____

_____

favorite Part of Today

_____

_____

_____

_____

Improvement for Tomorrow

_____

_____

_____

_____

Today's *Intention*

_____

_____

_____

Daily *Gratitude*

_____

_____

_____

Self *Love* Compliment

_____

_____

_____

favorite Part of Today

_____

_____

_____

Improvement for Tomorrow

_____

_____

_____

_____

QUOTE: "Feeling calm means
that I am aligned."

232

Today's *Intention*

_____

_____

_____

_____

Daily *Gratitude*

_____

_____

_____

_____

Self *Love* Compliment

_____

_____

_____

_____

favorite Part of Today

_____

_____

_____

_____

Improvement for Tomorrow

_____

_____

_____

_____

Today's *Intention*

_____

_____

_____

_____

Daily *Gratitude*

_____

_____

_____

_____

Self *Love* Compliment

_____

_____

_____

_____

Favorite Part of Today

_____

_____

_____

_____

Improvement for Tomorrow

_____

_____

_____

_____

HAPPY TASK: Listen to a guided meditation.

234

Today's *Intention*

_____

_____

_____

_____

Daily *Gratitude*

_____

_____

_____

_____

Self *Love* Compliment

_____

_____

_____

_____

Favorite Part of Today

_____

_____

_____

_____

Improvement for Tomorrow

_____

_____

_____

_____

Today's *Intention*

_____
_____
_____
_____

Daily *Gratitude*

_____
_____
_____
_____

Self *Love* Compliment

_____
_____
_____
_____

favorite Part of Today

_____
_____
_____
_____

Improvement for Tomorrow

_____
_____
_____
_____

AFFIRMATION: "I am self-motivated."

236

Today's *Intention*

_____

_____

_____

Daily *Gratitude*

_____

_____

_____

Self *Love* Compliment

_____

_____

_____

favorite Part of Today

_____

_____

_____

Improvement for Tomorrow

_____

_____

_____

List a moment you faced a fear and were proud of yourself – regardless of how big or small it was. The only thing that matters is you did it.

_____
_____
_____
_____
_____
_____
_____
_____
_____
_____
_____
_____
_____
_____
_____
_____
_____
_____
_____

"I *learned* the power of my voice and how I could cast *spells* into the sky."

DATE: / /

Today's *Intention*
_____
_____
_____
_____

Daily *Gratitude*
_____
_____
_____
_____

Self *Love* Compliment
_____
_____
_____
_____

Favorite Part of Today
_____
_____
_____
_____

Improvement for Tomorrow
_____
_____
_____
_____

HAPPY TASK: Hug a tree.

240

Today's *Intention*

_____

_____

_____

_____

Daily *Gratitude*

_____

_____

_____

_____

Self *Love* **Compliment**

_____

_____

_____

_____

favorite **Part of Today**

_____

_____

_____

_____

Improvement **for Tomorrow**

_____

_____

_____

_____

Today's *Intention*

_____

_____

_____

_____

Daily *Gratitude*

_____

_____

_____

_____

Self *Love* **Compliment**

_____

_____

_____

_____

favorite **Part of Today**

_____

_____

_____

_____

Improvement **for Tomorrow**

_____

_____

_____

_____

Today's *Intention*

_____

_____

_____

_____

Daily *Gratitude*

_____

_____

_____

_____

Self *Love* **Compliment**

_____

_____

_____

_____

favorite **Part of Today**

_____

_____

_____

_____

Improvement **for Tomorrow**

_____

_____

_____

_____

AFFIRMATION: "I am lovable."

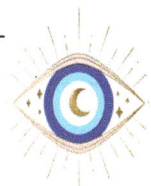

Today's *Intention*

_____
_____
_____
_____

Daily *Gratitude*

_____
_____
_____
_____

Self *Love* Compliment

_____
_____
_____
_____

favorite Part of Today

_____
_____
_____
_____

Improvement for Tomorrow

_____
_____
_____
_____

Today's *Intention*

_____

_____

_____

_____

Daily *Gratitude*

_____

_____

_____

_____

Self *Love* **Compliment**

_____

_____

_____

_____

favorite **Part of Today**

_____

_____

_____

_____

Improvement **for Tomorrow**

_____

_____

_____

_____

Today's *Intention*

_____

_____

_____

_____

Daily *Gratitude*

_____

_____

_____

_____

Self *Love* **Compliment**

_____

_____

_____

_____

Favorite **Part of Today**

_____

_____

_____

_____

Improvement **for Tomorrow**

_____

_____

_____

_____

QUOTE: "I make the best out of every situation."

246

"Be quiet, you have nothing to prove to anyone."

Express *Yourself*

Today's *Intention*

_____

_____

_____

_____

Daily *Gratitude*

_____

_____

_____

_____

Self *Love* Compliment

_____

_____

_____

_____

Favorite Part of Today

_____

_____

_____

_____

Improvement for Tomorrow

_____

_____

_____

_____

Today's *Intention*

_____
_____
_____
_____

Daily *Gratitude*

_____
_____
_____
_____

Self *Love* Compliment

_____
_____
_____
_____

favorite Part of Today

_____
_____
_____
_____

Improvement for Tomorrow

_____
_____
_____
_____

AFFIRMATION: "I surrender my worries
so I can flow in abundance."

Today's *Intention*

_____

_____

_____

Daily *Gratitude*

_____

_____

_____

Self *Love* Compliment

_____

_____

_____

favorite Part of Today

_____

_____

_____

Improvement for Tomorrow

_____

_____

_____

Today's *Intention*

_____

_____

_____

_____

Daily *Gratitude*

_____

_____

_____

_____

Self *Love* Compliment

_____

_____

_____

_____

favorite Part of Today

_____

_____

_____

_____

Improvement for Tomorrow

_____

_____

_____

_____

HAPPY TASK: Watch the sunset.

Today's *Intention*

_____

_____

_____

_____

Daily *Gratitude*

_____

_____

_____

_____

Self *Love* **Compliment**

_____

_____

_____

_____

favorite **Part of Today**

_____

_____

_____

_____

Improvement **for Tomorrow**

_____

_____

_____

_____

Today's *Intention*

_____

_____

_____

_____

Daily *Gratitude*

_____

_____

_____

_____

Self *Love* Compliment

_____

_____

_____

_____

favorite Part of Today

_____

_____

_____

_____

Improvement for Tomorrow

_____

_____

_____

_____

QUOTE: "My words transform
my reality."

254

Today's *Intention*

_____
_____
_____
_____

Daily *Gratitude*

_____
_____
_____
_____

Self *Love* Compliment

_____
_____
_____
_____

favorite Part of Today

_____
_____
_____
_____

Improvement for Tomorrow

_____
_____
_____
_____

255

Peppermint
Awareness

Did you know peppermint can also help you stay focused and alert throughout the day? Think about popping a mint in your mouth or bringing a peppermint plant to your office.

"Focus on *understanding* people versus judging them."

Today's *Intention*

_____

_____

_____

_____

Daily *Gratitude*

_____

_____

_____

_____

Self *Love* Compliment

_____

_____

_____

_____

Favorite Part of Today

_____

_____

_____

_____

Improvement for Tomorrow

_____

_____

_____

_____

AFFIRMATION: "I am exactly where I'm
supposed to be right now."

258

DATE: /   /

Today's *Intention*

_____
_____
_____
_____

Daily *Gratitude*

_____
_____
_____
_____

Self *Love* Compliment

_____
_____
_____
_____

favorite Part of Today

_____
_____
_____
_____

Improvement for Tomorrow

_____
_____
_____
_____

DATE: / /

Today's *Intention*

_____
_____
_____
_____

Daily *Gratitude*

_____
_____
_____
_____

Self *Love* Compliment

_____
_____
_____
_____

favorite Part of Today

_____
_____
_____
_____

Improvement for Tomorrow

_____
_____
_____
_____

Today's *Intention*

_____
_____
_____

Daily *Gratitude*

_____
_____
_____

Self *Love* Compliment

_____
_____
_____

favorite Part of Today

_____
_____
_____

Improvement for Tomorrow

_____
_____
_____

HAPPY TASK: Buy yourself some
fresh flowers.

Today's *Intention*

_____
_____
_____
_____

Daily *Gratitude*

_____
_____
_____
_____

Self *Love* Compliment

_____
_____
_____
_____

favorite Part of Today

_____
_____
_____
_____

Improvement for Tomorrow

_____
_____
_____
_____

DATE: / /

Today's *Intention*

_____
_____
_____
_____

Daily *Gratitude*

_____
_____
_____
_____

Self *Love* Compliment

_____
_____
_____
_____

favorite Part of Today

_____
_____
_____
_____

Improvement for Tomorrow

_____
_____
_____
_____

263

Today's *Intention*

_____

_____

_____

_____

Daily *Gratitude*

_____

_____

_____

_____

Self *Love* **Compliment**

_____

_____

_____

_____

Favorite **Part of Today**

_____

_____

_____

_____

Improvement **for Tomorrow**

_____

_____

_____

_____

AFFIRMATION: "I am brave."

264

"When you don't *know* what to do, be still, and breathe. The *solution* will then be able to reach you."

Doodle what's on your mind right now.

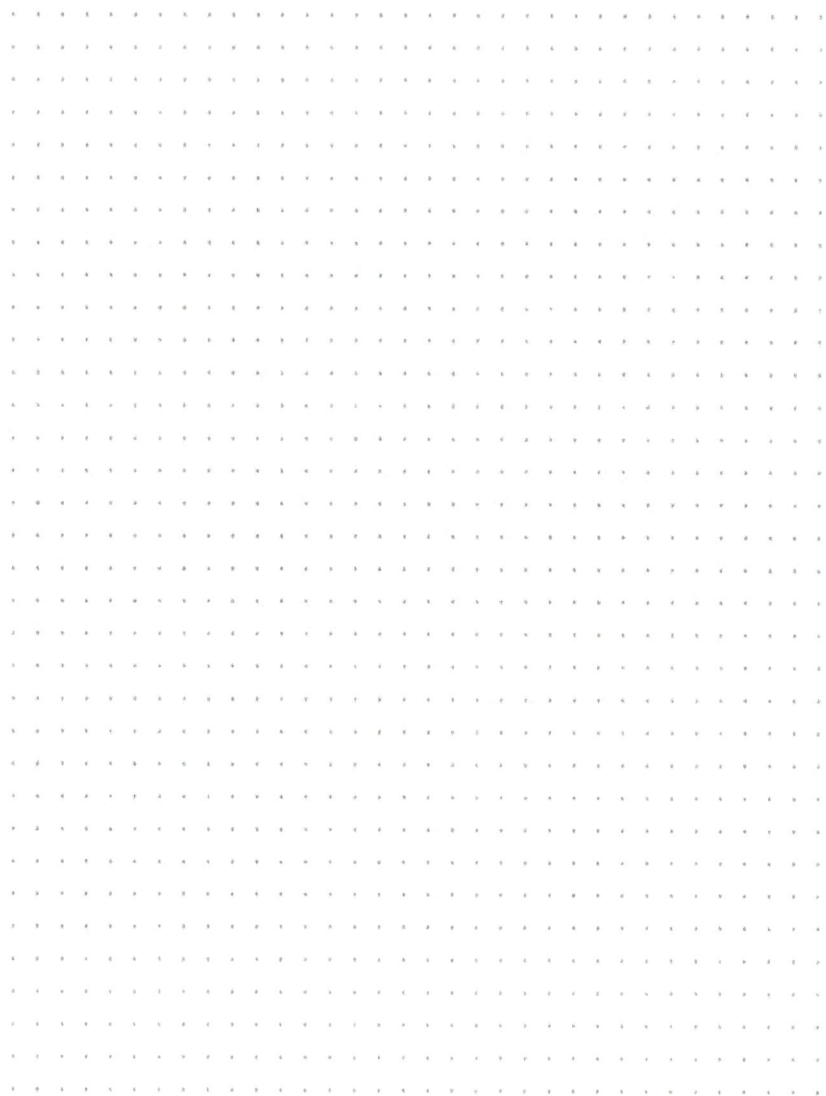

Today's *Intention*

_____
_____
_____
_____

Daily *Gratitude*

_____
_____
_____
_____

Self *Love* Compliment

_____
_____
_____
_____

favorite Part of Today

_____
_____
_____
_____

Improvement for Tomorrow

_____
_____
_____
_____

267

Today's *Intention*

_____

_____

_____

_____

Daily *Gratitude*

_____

_____

_____

_____

Self *Love* Compliment

_____

_____

_____

_____

favorite Part of Today

_____

_____

_____

_____

Improvement for Tomorrow

_____

_____

_____

_____

HAPPY TASK: Walk around your home and scan
the energy. Is there one part that feels
heavier than another? Which part is it?
Is it time to organize that area?

Today's *Intention*

_____

_____

_____

_____

Daily *Gratitude*

_____

_____

_____

_____

Self *Love* Compliment

_____

_____

_____

_____

favorite Part of Today

_____

_____

_____

_____

Improvement for Tomorrow

_____

_____

_____

_____

269

Today's *Intention*

_____

_____

_____

_____

Daily *Gratitude*

_____

_____

_____

_____

Self *Love* Compliment

_____

_____

_____

_____

favorite Part of Today

_____

_____

_____

_____

Improvement for Tomorrow

_____

_____

_____

_____

AFFIRMATION: "I surrender my worries
so I can flow in abundance."

Today's *Intention*

_____

_____

_____

_____

Daily *Gratitude*

_____

_____

_____

_____

Self *Love* Compliment

_____

_____

_____

_____

favorite Part of Today

_____

_____

_____

_____

Improvement for Tomorrow

_____

_____

_____

_____

Today's *Intention*

_____
_____
_____
_____

Daily *Gratitude*

_____
_____
_____
_____

Self *Love* Compliment

_____
_____
_____
_____

favorite Part of Today

_____
_____
_____
_____

Improvement for Tomorrow

_____
_____
_____
_____

AFFIRMATION: "I unleash my wild this week and have more fun."

DATE: / /

Today's *Intention*

_____
_____
_____
_____

Daily *Gratitude*

_____
_____
_____
_____

Self *Love* Compliment

_____
_____
_____
_____

favorite Part of Today

_____
_____
_____
_____

Improvement for Tomorrow

_____
_____
_____
_____

273

The best *compass* is my heart

SELF CARE CHECK-IN

What is something positive about yourself that you like?

_____

_____

_____

_____

_____

_____

_____

_____

_____

"I sat by the *water* so it could teach me how to *flow* again."

Today's *Intention*

_____
_____
_____
_____

Daily *Gratitude*

_____
_____
_____
_____

Self *Love* Compliment

_____
_____
_____
_____

Favorite Part of Today

_____
_____
_____
_____

Improvement for Tomorrow

_____
_____
_____
_____

HAPPY TASK: Write out 3 ways you
can understand people first before
judging them.

276

Today's *Intention*

_____
_____
_____
_____

Daily *Gratitude*

_____
_____
_____
_____

Self *Love* Compliment

_____
_____
_____
_____

favorite Part of Today

_____
_____
_____
_____

Improvement for Tomorrow

_____
_____
_____
_____

277

Today's *Intention*

_____
_____
_____
_____

Daily *Gratitude*

_____
_____
_____
_____

Self *Love* Compliment

_____
_____
_____
_____

favorite Part of Today

_____
_____
_____
_____

Improvement for Tomorrow

_____
_____
_____
_____

Today's *Intention*

_____

_____

_____

_____

Daily *Gratitude*

_____

_____

_____

_____

Self *Love* Compliment

_____

_____

_____

_____

favorite Part of Today

_____

_____

_____

_____

Improvement for Tomorrow

_____

_____

_____

_____

AFFIRMATION: "I am enough."

Today's *Intention*

_____

_____

_____

_____

Daily *Gratitude*

_____

_____

_____

_____

Self *Love* Compliment

_____

_____

_____

_____

Favorite Part of Today

_____

_____

_____

_____

Improvement for Tomorrow

_____

_____

_____

_____

Today's *Intention*

_____
_____
_____
_____

Daily *Gratitude*

_____
_____
_____
_____

Self *Love* Compliment

_____
_____
_____

favorite Part of Today

_____
_____
_____
_____

Improvement for Tomorrow

_____
_____
_____
_____

Today's *Intention*

_____

_____

_____

_____

Daily *Gratitude*

_____

_____

_____

_____

Self *Love* Compliment

_____

_____

_____

_____

Favorite Part of Today

_____

_____

_____

_____

Improvement for Tomorrow

_____

_____

_____

_____

QUOTE: "Small actions lead to
big results."

282

"Be *detached* from the outcome and enjoy the process. As long as you are *creating* with inspiration, that energy will make it *successful*."

Ex it Out!

Pawn or donate old gifts from exes if you are trying to attract a new relationship. Toss out memories that carry a block.

Make a list of what to let go:

_____

_____

_____

_____

_____

_____

_____

_____

Today's *Intention*

_____
_____
_____

Daily *Gratitude*

_____
_____
_____

Self *Love* Compliment

_____
_____
_____

favorite Part of Today

_____
_____
_____

Improvement for Tomorrow

_____
_____
_____

Today's *Intention*

_____

_____

_____

_____

Daily *Gratitude*

_____

_____

_____

_____

Self *Love* Compliment

_____

_____

_____

_____

Favorite Part of Today

_____

_____

_____

_____

Improvement for Tomorrow

_____

_____

_____

_____

POSITIVE ENERGY TIP: Rearrange small
things to change the flow of energy.
Things like books, plants, or frames.   286

Today's *Intention*

_____
_____
_____
_____

Daily *Gratitude*

_____
_____
_____
_____

Self *Love* Compliment

_____
_____
_____
_____

favorite Part of Today

_____
_____
_____
_____

Improvement for Tomorrow

_____
_____
_____
_____

Today's *Intention*

_____

_____

_____

_____

Daily *Gratitude*

_____

_____

_____

_____

Self *Love* Compliment

_____

_____

_____

_____

favorite Part of Today

_____

_____

_____

_____

Improvement for Tomorrow

_____

_____

_____

_____

AFFIRMATION: "I am playful and I radiate joy."

Today's *Intention*

Daily *Gratitude*

Self *Love* Compliment

---

favorite Part of Today

Improvement for Tomorrow

Today's *Intention*

_____

_____

_____

Daily *Gratitude*

_____

_____

_____

Self *Love* **Compliment**

_____

_____

_____

favorite **Part of Today**

_____

_____

_____

Improvement **for Tomorrow**

_____

_____

_____

_____

SELF-CARE CHECK IN: What are you
most proud of today?

Today's *Intention*

_____

_____

_____

_____

Daily *Gratitude*

_____

_____

_____

_____

Self *Love* Compliment

_____

_____

_____

_____

favorite Part of Today

_____

_____

_____

_____

Improvement for Tomorrow

_____

_____

_____

_____

I love little me and make her *proud*.

SELF CARE CHECK-IN

List 5 compliments you can give your "inner child" now. What are some things you admire about the kid you once were?

_____

_____

_____

_____

_____

_____

_____

_____

_____

"The only way to *heal* is to feel."

"And just like that, she *walked* away from who she no longer *wanted* to be and into who she always *dreamed* of becoming."

Congratulations

You have completed the *Abundance* Journal

What's changed from when
you started to now?

_____

_____

_____

_____

_____

_____

Leave A Review:

I would love to know your thoughts on how the
Annie The Alchemist Abundance Journal helped you.
Leave me a review wherever you purchased the book
so we can connect further and continue to inspire
others to believe in the power of journaling.

Acknowledgments

George + Carmen, thank you for your pure love, continual inspiration and for believing in me. I love you both infinitely.

Art, George, Mia and AJ for your presence, encouragement and supporting my spirit as a writer.

Annie The Alchemist followers for your energy, kindness and our morning rituals and meditations.

To all who have supported My Little Prayer Book: 75 Prayers, Poems & Mantras For Illumination, your support helped me complete the journal.

Elmo + Petunia, thank you for your unconditional love, pug snuggles and kisses. My babies.

My dear friends and those I call sisters, thank you for believing in my creative ideas and helping me arrive here. I'm grateful to walk the journey with you all.

Lauren, thank you for being my friend and helping me trust in divine timing with this journal.

Taimara, thank you for holding the candle up high during the time it took to complete this.

Flor Ana, thank you for your mentorship and helping me finish what I started with so much light.

Indie Earth, thank you for publishing this journal.

All readers who find light in these pages.

Other Products

Annie has many products to compliment your ABUNDANCE JOURNAL. Check out her:

AFFIRMATIONS FOR ABUNDANCE DECK

MY LITTLE PRAYER BOOK: 75 PRAYERS, POEMS & MANTRAS FOR ILLUMINATION

Available on Amazon.com

About the Author

Annie Vazquez is a poet, writer and former journalist, featured in the Miami Herald, Refinery29, NBC6. and Good Morning America. Annie is certified by Deepak Chopra's Chopra Meditation School, and she is certified in reiki and sound bowl. Her shop, Annie The Alchemist, has been featured on People Espanol, Elite Daily, Latin Biz, Parents and Time Out Magazine. Annie has published a variety of ebooks on self-love and wellness and has created a bestselling affirmation desk titled Affirmations for Abundance. In 2023, she released My Little Prayer Book: 75 Prayers, Poems & Mantras For Illumination, a non-denominational guide book that brings answers, comfort and helps you peacefully manifest your goals. When Annie is not writing, she is hanging out with her BFFs, Elmo and Petunia, and traveling the world.

Connect with Annie on Instagram:
@anniethealchemist / @thefashionpoet / @anniewriteswords

www.annievazquez.com

9 798989 555161